Eric

If I Knew Then, What I Know Now!
College and Financial Aid Planning

From A Parent's
Perspective Workbook

If you do not want to pay full price for college, you need a plan! This workbook will help parents, guardians, aunts, uncles, godparents, organizations, anyone who assists middle and high school students, create a college and scholarship game plan to cut the cost of college tuition!

Cynthia Hammond Davis

Contents

Introduction

I am so excited about this workbook! Parents need an action plan and this workbook will help bring all the pieces of the college and scholarship planning puzzle together. This workbook should be used along with my book, *If I Knew Then What I Know Now! College and Financial Aid Planning From A Parent's Perspective.* In the book I share my story. I want you to learn from my mistakes. I want you to start earlier than I did because junior and senior year is entirely too late to start looking for colleges and scholarships! This book has been written with the middle and high school parent/guardian in mind. Actually, college and career planning should start shortly after parents find out they're expecting a child. Colleges are expensive and planning ahead should help you save a lot of money.

This workbook helps you create an action plan that you can alter as you go along. If you start early, you should have a great plan for your child. It takes years and years to get your child ready for college. Colleges want students who are not only excelling in the classroom, but also outside of the classroom and in their communities.

This workbook will show you what most colleges are looking for in a prospective student. It will show you how to make your child become the "need" for the institution. If your child meets the "need," most colleges will pay them with scholarships (free money) to attend.

This workbook helps you understand who your child is and what their interests, skills, abilities and talents are and how they can use these gifts in school, out of school, in college and in the workplace. If we do the things that interest us, are skilled at, and have the talent to do, I believe that we will stay in our careers a long time because we are working in fields that we are passionate about. This workbook will help you identify those skills in your child and assist them in perfecting them.

This workbook provides parents with questions they may not know to ask teachers, counselors and other staff to make sure their children are receiving the best school experience possible based on their individual needs.

This workbook tells you when you should search for scholarships and your role in this process. Parents must assist in this. If you are not available to provide assistance, find someone who you trust to help your child. It could be an older sibling, friend or relative. The first chapter is crucial. You need to build a team.

It is my hope that this workbook will be used every year until your child attends college. Please tell every parent you know about this workbook and the book!

Cynthia Hammond Davis

Read Chapter 1

Teamwork is The Key

Remember, as a family you are a team!

Name the key players on your team who are family members.

1 _____
2 _____
3 _____
4 _____
5 _____
6 _____

How does each person play a role in your child's life?

_____
_____
_____
_____
_____
_____
_____
_____
_____
_____
_____
_____
_____
_____
_____
_____

Name key players on your team who are in your community, places of worship, or other organizations, sports or other activities/ programs.

1 _____
2 _____
3 _____
4 _____
5 _____
6 _____

How does each person play a role in your child's life?

_____
_____
_____
_____
_____
_____
_____
_____
_____
_____
_____
_____
_____
_____

Name key players at your child's school, other parents or parent organizations.

1 _____
2 _____
3 _____
4 _____
5 _____
6 _____
7 _____
8 _____

How does each person play a role in your child's life?

_____
_____
_____
_____
_____
_____
_____
_____
_____
_____
_____
_____
_____
_____
_____
_____
_____

Speak with your child's teachers monthly through email or in person if necessary. How are they doing?

_____
_____
_____
_____
_____
_____
_____
_____
_____
_____
_____
_____
_____
_____

What's your plan? What did you learn from this section?
Where, or with whom, do you need to talk to in this section? Explain and write your next steps.

_____
_____
_____
_____
_____
_____
_____
_____
_____
_____
_____
_____
_____
_____
_____
_____
_____
_____
_____
_____
_____

Please respond to the following questions to assess your involvement with your child's high school.

Key Points	Responses
Did you attend back-to-school night this academic year?	☐ Yes　☐ No
Did you attend the grade-level meeting this academic year?	☐ Yes　☐ No
Are you a member of the school's PTA or PTSA?	☐ Yes　☐ No
If yes, when was the last PTA or PTSA meeting you attended this academic year?	_____
Have you joined the parents' email group at school?	☐ Yes　☐ No
Do you participate in school activities that involve your child?	☐ Yes　☐ No
Have you volunteered at your child's school this academic year?	☐ Yes　☐ No
Do you have online access to your child's grades? Check with school staff to see if online access is available.	☐ Yes　☐ No
How often do you check your child's grades?	☐ Regularly ☐ Occasionally ☐ Never
Are you comfortable talking to teachers about your child?	☐ Yes　☐ No
When was the last conference you had with your child's teacher?	_____
How often do you email your child's teachers?	☐ Regularly ☐ Occasionally ☐ Never
Have you met with your child's Counselor this year?	☐ Yes　☐ No
Have you met with your child's College Counselor, if the school has one?	_____
How often do you visit your child's high school website?	☐ Regularly ☐ Occasionally ☐ Never

This section has been provided courtesy of Dr. Stephanie Mbella, author of, "The Immigrant Guide to the American Educational System."

Additional Notes:

_____

_____

_____

_____

_____

_____

_____

_____

_____

_____

_____

_____

_____

_____

_____

_____

_____

_____

Additional Notes:

_____

_____

_____

_____

_____

_____

_____

_____

_____

_____

_____

_____

_____

_____

_____

_____

_____

Read Chapter 2

Finding your Child's Gifts/Talents, Abilities, Strengths & Passion

This chapter is so important when trying to figure out what your child might want to pursue as a career.

Watch your child closely. What are they doing? Write it down.

_____
_____
_____
_____
_____
_____
_____
_____
_____
_____
_____

What are your child's skills, abilities, talents as you see them?

_____
_____
_____
_____
_____
_____
_____
_____

What do you find them engaged in, or doing, in their spare time?

_____
_____
_____
_____
_____
_____
_____
_____

What are your child's strengths? Explain.

_____
_____
_____
_____
_____
_____
_____
_____
_____
_____

What are your child's weaknesses? Explain.

_____
_____
_____
_____
_____
_____
_____
_____
_____
_____
_____
_____

Does she/he need a tutor? If so, call the counseling department for a list of tutors. Are teachers available for tutoring during the day? Some schools have peer/student tutors. Write them in this book and follow through with it.

_____
_____
_____
_____
_____
_____
_____
_____

In what subjects does your child excel? Math, English, Science, Art, Music, Athletics, Other?

_____
_____
_____
_____
_____
_____
_____

Ask teachers and counselors what opportunities are available for students who excel in a subject. Write down their answers and follow up on it.

_____
_____
_____
_____
_____
_____
_____
_____

Is your child enrolled in Honors AP or IB courses (Advanced Placement/College Level, International Baccalaureate), if available?

_____
_____
_____
_____
_____
_____
_____
_____

How many books did your child read this month at home? Did you see him/her reading? Try to find books that match their interests.

_____
_____
_____
_____
_____
_____
_____

Have them write down, or type, some of the chapters in the book they have read just to get in the habit of reading and writing/typing. They will read and write/type a lot in college.

What's your plan? What did you learn from this section?
Where, or with whom, do you need to talk to in this section? Explain and write your next steps.

_____
_____
_____
_____
_____
_____
_____
_____

This section has been provided courtesy of Dr. Stephanie Mbella, author of, "The Immigrant Guide to the American Educational System."

How to Choose a College Major and Career.
There are a multitude of ways to select a college major that will lead you to a career.

1. *Interests*

In this case, major selection focuses on things one loves doing. One of the most common methods used in educational settings and that students and parents can explore on their own is the Holland personality codes. According to Dr. John Holland, who devised this theory, people can fall under six categories of occupations: Realistic – Investigative – Artistic – Social – Enterprising – Conventional. The short acronym of this approach is RIASEC. Holland codes can be used to explore potential college majors. During the college selection process, educators encourage students to complete a Holland Code career assessment to provide them with an overview of career clusters based on interests. Some tests are available online for free and the results allow the student to explore the breadth of careers deriving from a specific major. Generally, RIASEC personality tests use Likert-style questions with students rating different tasks from the most enjoyable to the least enjoyable. After securing a list of careers from the RIASEC test, a student can examine their future job outlook. There are jobs that have been present in the labor market for centuries. But as students explore their career outlook, they can examine new trends in the job market to determine what career would be the most likely to satisfy them in the future. Students might consider a specific career as they explore and enter college. However, as they delve more in their studies, they might change their mind, especially if they want to pursue graduate studies or embrace a professional field such as medicine and law. As an illustration, a graduating high school senior wants to become a teacher and for that purpose, he majors in both Mathematics and Computer Science. As he progresses in his studies, he explores career opportunities, future job outlook, and potential lifetime earnings. After his research, his focus shifts from the field of education to finance. He can use his background in mathematics and computer science to work as a broker or a Wall Street trader.

Some majors offered in a community college setting enable students to immediately join the workforce upon completion. Examples include automotive, nursing, construction, paralegal studies and accounting. Holders of an Associate Degree in one of those fields can choose to continue their education by earning a Bachelor's Degree, or may choose to seek promotion opportunities within their jobs.

Holland Code	Sample 2-year College Majors	Sample 4-year College Majors
REALISTIC *"The Doers"* *Who are they?* *People who have athletic or mechanical abilities prefer to work with objects, machines, tools, plants, or animals, or to be outdoors.* *What do they like?* *Tinker with machines/vehicles Work outdoors* *Use their hands* *Be physically active* *Build things* *Tend to, or train, animals* *Work on electronic equipment*	*Architectural Technology* *Automotive Service Specialist* *Computer Technology* *Computer Science* *Construction Technology* *Criminal Justice: Police Option* *Engineering & Technology:* *Fire Protection Technology* *Horticulture* *Landscape Development* *Manufacturing* *Physical Therapist Assistant*	*Aerospace Engineering* *Architectural Technology* *Aviation* *Civil Engineering Technology* *Computer Engineering* *Computer Network Administration* *Computer Science* *Computer Software Specialist* *Construction Engineering Technology* *Construction Science* *Dental Hygiene*

INVESTIGATIVE	American Sign Language	Area Studies
"The Thinkers"	Health Information Technology	Anthropology
Who are they?	Medical Assisting	Astronomy
People who like to observe, learn,	Nursing	Astrophysics
investigate, analyze, evaluate or solve	Occupational Therapy Assistant	Biochemistry
problems.	Veterinary Science Technology	Bioengineering
		Biology
What do they like to do?		Botany
Explore a variety of ideas		Chemical Engineering
Use computers,		Chemistry
Work independently		Civil Engineering
Perform lab experiments		Computer Science & Engineering
Read scientific or technical journals		Criminology
Analyze data		Dentistry
deal with abstractions		Economics
Do research & be challenged		Electrical Engineering
		Environmental Sciences
		Foreign Languages
		Linguistics
		Nursing (all programs)
		Pharmacy
		Physics
		Pre-Medicine
		Pre-Dentistry
		Pre-Veterinary Medicine
		Psychology
		Sociology
		Veterinarian medicine
		Women's and Gender Studies
		Zoology
Holland Code	***Sample 2-year College Majors***	***Sample 4-year College Majors***
ARTISTIC	Communications and Media Arts	Architecture
"The Creators"	Fine Arts	Art
	Graphic Design	Art Education
	Interior Design	Art History
Who are they?	Photographic Imaging	Dance
People who have artistic, innovating	Radio and Television Production	Drama
or intuition abilities and like to work	Technical Communication	English
in unstructured situations using their	Performing Arts: Drama	English Education
imagination and creativity.	Performing Arts: Music	Environmental Design
		Ethics and Religion
		Film/Video
What do they like to do?		Foreign Language Education
Attend concerts, theatres, and art exhibit		Humanities
		Journalism and Mass Communication

Read fiction, plays, and poetry, Work on crafts Take photographs Express themselves creatively. Deal with ambiguous ideas		Journalism: Broadcasting & Electronic Media Library-Media Education Linguistics Music Music Education Philosophy Religious Studies Theatre
SOCIAL "The Helpers" Who are they? People who like to work with people to enlighten, inform, help. What do they like? Work in groups, Help people with problems Participate in meetings Do volunteer work Work with young people Play team sports Serve others	Community Service Assistant Community/Outdoor Recreation Human Resources Mgmt. Recreation Leadership Travel & Tourism	Athletic Training Career & Technical Education Community Health Communication Disorders Criminal Justice Emergency Medical Science Technology Health and Exercise History Institutional Health Care Kinesiotherapy Nutrition Physical Education Physical Therapy Public Administration Science Education Social Studies Education Social Work Speech Language Pathology Special Education Therapeutic Recreation

Holland Code	Sample 2-year College Majors	Sample 4-year College Majors
ENTERPRISING "The Decision Makers" Who are they? People who like to work with people, influencing, persuading, performing, leading or managing for organizational goals or economic gain. What do they like? Make decisions affecting others	Accounting Banking Sequence Business Administration Business Management Finance Insurance Management Marketing Office Management Real Estate Restaurant Management Retail Business Management	Business Administration Business Management Technology Electronic Commerce Entrepreneurship/Family & Small Business Finance Human Resource Management Industrial Engineering International Business Management Marketing Marketing & Sales Technology Operations

Be elected to office Win a leadership or sales award Start their own service or business Campaign politically Meet important people Have power or status		Management Public Relations Pre-Law Public Affairs & Administration Public Affairs & Community Services Purchasing Urban Studies
CONVENTIONAL *"The organizers"* *Who are they?* *People who like to work with data, have clerical or numerical ability, carry out tasks in detail, or follow through on others' instructions.* *What do they like?* *Follow clearly defined procedures* *Use data processing equipment, Work with numbers* *Be responsible for details* *Collect or organize things*	*Computer Information Systems* *Food Service Administration* *Medical Records* *Paralegal Studies*	*Accounting* *Accounting Technology* *Administrative Office Technology* *Data Processing* *Economics* *Financial Services* *Information Systems* *Information Services and Support* *Legal Assisting/Pre-Law Studies* *Logistics & Management* *Management Information Systems* *Paralegal Studies* *Transportation Management Technology*

Source: www.iseek.org and the University of Oklahoma Career Services

2. *Skills*

Students have to determine what they do well or competencies which they have an affinity or aptitude for. Innate or acquired through practice, talents can serve as guides for a major selection. For this purpose, they can be broken into three groups:

- *People skills: serving, helping, speaking, negotiating, persuading, mentoring, supervising*
- *Data skills: computing, analyzing, synthetizing, forecasting*
- *"Things" skills: operating, fixing, setting up, handling, controlling*

3. *Values*

Values are developed from an early age and are a reflection of what one holds as important in life. They are dynamic in the sense that they can be shaped and re-shaped by our experiences. Similar to skills, they can help a student figure out their college major and careers derived therefrom. The aim at this point is to know what is important to you, the student.

- *Personal and family values: some majors lead to careers granting more time and flexibility to spend time with families.*
- *Cultural or religious values: for some people, religion plays an important role in their life. Therefore, it would be somehow improbable for a conservative Christian to thrive in a job advocating abortion or euthanasia (assisted-suicide).*
- *Economic values: if financial status is vital for a student, he or she should look into majors yielding some of the highest incomes on the pay scale. The U.S. Bureau of Labor Statistics is a great resource in that regard.*

4. *Personality*

It is the way you have been from birth. In terms of personality, two types emerge. Either one is extrovert or an introvert. Knowing their personality type can help students narrow down their choices of college majors. Commonly, the results of the Myer Briggs Personality Test provide students an insight into who they are.

Sources of Energy	E	Extrovert *Attention is focused on the outer world of people and things*	I	Introvert *Attention is focused on the inner world of thoughts and reflections*
Information Acquisition	S	Sensing *Information is processed through the five senses (sight, hearing, taste, smell, and touch)*	N	Intuition *Information is processed through a hunch or "sixth sense"*
Decision Making	T	Thinking *Decisions are based on logic and impartial/objective analysis*	F	Feeling *Decisions are based on people and subjective in value*
Orientation towards the Outer World	J	Judging *Lifestyle is planned, organized, and decisive*	P	Perceiving *Lifestyle is flexible, spontaneous, and adaptable*

Source: Myers Briggs Personality Test

The RIASEC TEST Student Worksheet

Completing this test/survey may help your child discover his/her career path based on likes. Interests, skills, etc.

Read each statement. If you agree with the statement, circle the appropriate box. There are no wrong answers! Record your scores in the appropriate box at the bottom of the table to know some of your career pathways.

	1	2	3	4	5	6
A	I like to work on cars.	I like to do puzzles.	I am good at working independently.	I like to work in teams.	I am an ambitious person.	I like to organize things (files, desks).
B	I like to build things.	I like to do experiments.	I like to draw.	I like to teach or train people.	I like to try to influence or persuade other people.	I like to have clear instructions to follow.
C	I like to take care of animals.	I enjoy science.	I enjoy creative writing.	I like trying to help people solve their problems.	I like selling things.	I wouldn't mind working 8 hours per day in an office.
D	I like putting things together or assemble things.	I enjoy trying to figure out how things work.	I like to read about art and music.	I am interested in healing people.	I am quick to take on new responsibilities.	I pay attention to details.
E	I like to cook.	I like to analyze things (problems/ situations).	I like to play instruments or sing.	I enjoy learning about other cultures.	I would like to start my own business.	I like to do filing or typing.
F	I am a practical person.	I like working with numbers or charts.	I like acting in plays.	I like to get into discussions about issues.	I like to lead.	I am good at keeping records of my work.
G	I like working outdoors.	I'm good at math.	I am a creative person.	I like helping people.	I like to give speeches.	I would like to work in an office.
	R	I	A	S	E	C	← Total

My Highest 3 Codes are: _____   _____   _____

Source: Hawaii Public Schools and Ohio Adult Basic and Literacy Education (ABLE) Program

Additional Notes:

_____

_____

_____

_____

_____

_____

_____

_____

_____

_____

_____

_____

_____

_____

_____

_____

_____

_____

_____

_____

Additional Notes:

_____

_____

_____

_____

_____

_____

_____

_____

_____

_____

_____

_____

_____

_____

_____

_____

_____

Read Chapter 3

The Importance of Good Grades and SAT/ACT Scores

Students may start taking the mock PSAT (Practice SAT) as early as 9th grade. Eleventh Grade students will take the official PSAT (Practice SAT) in October to compete for the National Merit Scholarship Qualifier. This test is normally taken at the student's school. Some schools pay for the test, but some schools do not. Check with your child's school in September.

You can study for the test AND other K-12 subjects using Khanacademy.org. It's FREE! You can donate if you'd like, but it' FREE!

Students can take the official SAT in high school, but most school counselors suggest students complete Algebra 2 before taking it. It's totally up to you. What subjects (Math, Reading, English, (Science-ACT)) will your child need additional support in as it pertains to the SAT or ACT?

_____

_____

_____

_____

My child will sign up with khanacademy.org or another tutoring agency (by what date?).

_____

_____

_____

_____

My child will work on khanacademy.org or another tutoring agency (how many days per week?).

_____

_____

_____

_____

My child worked on khanacademy.org or another tutoring agency _____ times this month.

_____

_____

_____

_____

_____

Did your child find khanacademy.org or another PSAT or SAT prep/practice helpful?

_____

_____

_____

Parents, have grades improved since tutoring or PSAT, SAT/ACT practice began?

_____

_____

_____

_____

The next set of questions are for <u>High School Students ONLY</u> who are taking the official SAT or ACT

When will you take the official test?

_____

_____

_____

_____

Look on Collegeboard.org or ACT.org to see when you need to register for the test you will take.

What's the deadline date to register?

_____

_____

_____

_____

How much will it cost to register?

_____

_____

_____

_____

Is my child eligible for a fee waiver? (Check with your counselor)

_____

_____

_____

_____

Will my school pay for an SAT test? If so, for what grade? What's the date of the free test?

_____

_____

_____

_____

To what colleges will your child send their scores when they register for the test? It is suggested that you send ALL scores to your top four colleges. (If you wait until you receive the scores, you will have to pay $13 or more to send the scores to each college.)

_____

_____

_____

_____

What days will your child practice for the test? What time?

_____
_____
_____
_____
_____
_____

My child will receive practice from (khanacademy.org, or another organization or individual) Add the name of the organization or tutor & contact information here:

_____
_____
_____
_____
_____
_____

Look at college websites to see what the SAT or ACT scores are of students who have been accepted. Where does your child fit? (If your child will take the test again, use the same questions above).

_____
_____
_____
_____
_____
_____

Remember, not all colleges/universities consider SAT/ACT scores. Some colleges allow students to "opt-out." Check with fairtest.org to see which colleges provide this option. Temple University, Wake Forest, and Goucher College are some that come to mind, but make sure you check for other requirements and stipulations.

List the colleges that "opt-out" of the SAT/ACT that your child may consider:

_____
_____
_____
_____
_____

What's your plan? What did you learn from this section?
Where, or with whom, do you need to talk to in this section? Explain and write your next steps.

_____
_____
_____
_____
_____

College Planning Process

Student <u>Only</u> Worksheet

Planning ahead, answer the following questions to see where you stand compared to the other pool of applicants. If you need more space, use the Additional Notes section at the end of this chapter.

What Do Colleges Want?	Self- Reflection	What would you do to stand out among other applicants this year?
Challenging High School Curriculum ☐ Honors Classes ☐ AP Classes ☐ IB Classes ☐ College Classes	What rigorous classes have you taken?	_____
Strong G.P.A.	How would you rate your grades since 8 or 9th grade? (increasing, decreasing, constant)	_____
High standardized test scores	Did you earn college-ready scores on the SAT and/or ACT? (Ask your child's counselor.)	_____
A record of Community Services	What volunteering experiences did you have during which you made a difference in someone's life?	_____
Work or internship experience	What professional experience do you have?	_____
Quality involvement in activities	What leadership role have you held at school, in a community organization, or at work?	_____
Awards earned in High School	What awards have you earned in High School? (Honor roll, leadership, athletic, community, etc.)	_____
A well written essay	How would you characterize your writing skills? (Excellent? Good? Acceptable? Low?) Why?	_____
Positive recommendations from school staff and/or community members	If asked today, who are the three people <u>at your school and/or in your community</u> who would give you great recommendation letters for a college application?	_____

Source: Unknown author (2009). "Top 10 things colleges look for in a high school student." Retrieved from: http://school.familyeducation.com/collegeprep/high-school/56210.html This section has been provided courtesy of Dr. Stephanie Mbella, author of, "The Immigrant Guide to the American Educational System."

Parent and Student College Planning Worksheet
Please complete together to assess your child's college planning process.

Key Points	Available Options		
Grade level	□ 9th	□ 10th	□ 11th	□ 12th
Academics	Current unweighted GPA: _____ Current weighted GPA: _____		
	Honors classes taken	AP classes taken	IB classes taken
	_____	_____	_____
	_____	_____	_____
	_____	_____	_____
	_____	_____	_____
	_____	_____	_____
	_____	_____	_____
Extra-curricular activities starting from 9th Grade	Activity	Role/Position	Leadership position
	_____	_____	□ Yes □ No
	_____	_____	□ Yes □ No
	_____	_____	□ Yes □ No
	_____	_____	□ Yes □ No
	_____	_____	□ Yes □ No
	_____	_____	□ Yes □ No
	_____	_____	□ Yes □ No
	_____	_____	□ Yes □ No
Exposure to college environment (List events attended and/or schools visited)	College fairs	College tours	Open houses
	_____	_____	_____
	_____	_____	_____
	_____	_____	_____
	_____	_____	_____
Standardized test preparation	SAT Test		
	Test Date	Grade	College level scores
	_____	_____	□ Yes □ No
	_____	_____	□ Yes □ No
	_____	_____	□ Yes □ No
	ACT Test		
	Test Date	Grade	College level scores
	_____	_____	□ Yes □ No
	_____	_____	□ Yes □ No
	_____	_____	□ Yes □ No

This section has been provided courtesy of Dr. Stephanie Mbella, author of, "The Immigrant Guide to the American Educational

Additional notes:

Additional notes:

_____

_____

_____

_____

_____

_____

_____

_____

_____

_____

_____

_____

_____

_____

_____

_____

_____

_____

_____

Read Chapter 4

Extracurricular Activities, Community Service & Summer Opportunities

This information will help counselors and teachers write detailed recommendation letters and may also help with essay topics for college and scholarships. If you need more space to write, use the Additional Notes section at the end of this chapter.

What are your child's extracurricular activities?

_____
_____
_____
_____
_____
_____

What's your child's role? Explain in detail.

_____
_____
_____
_____
_____
_____
_____
_____

What community service activities is your child involved in (outside of church or religious organizations)?

_____
_____
_____
_____
_____
_____

What's your child's role? Explain in detail.

_____
_____
_____
_____

Summer Enrichment Programs, Clubs, Activities are crucial!

What's your child doing in the summer? Explain in detail.

_____

_____

_____

_____

_____

_____

_____

What's your plan? What did you learn from this section?
Where, or with whom, do you need to talk to in this section? Explain and write your next steps.

_____

_____

_____

_____

_____

_____

_____

_____

_____

_____

_____

_____

_____

_____

_____

_____

_____

_____

_____

_____

_____

_____

_____

_____

Additional Notes:

Additional Notes:

Read Chapter 5

NCAA (For Student Athletes)

What sport does your child play?

_____

_____

_____

_____

Is he or she interested in playing sports in college? If so, what division: I II or III? What's the difference between the divisions? If you are not sure, read Chapter 5 again.

_____

_____

_____

_____

Has your child registered for the NCAA Clearinghouse? If not, go to NCAA.Org Eligibility Center. Students can register as early as 10th or 11th grade. There is a one-time fee in order to register. Fee waivers are available for those who qualify. Check with your counselor or athletic director.

After registering for the NCAA Clearinghouse, go to the counseling department at your school to request your transcript be sent to the NCAA Clearinghouse.

Date your child requested his/her transcript be sent to the NCAA Clearinghouse:

_____

_____

_____

_____

Date your child sent his/her ACT/SAT scores to the NCAA Clearinghouse:

_____

_____

_____

_____

Your child's NCAA Clearinghouse Number is:

_____

_____

_____

_____

To see if your child is a good fit for the college team, go to a college website that has your child's sport. Look at the athletic roster of that sport.

Count the number of seniors on the team. (They may graduate before you arrive.)

_____
_____
_____
_____

Count the number of juniors on the team. (They may have one year left before they graduate.)

_____
_____
_____
_____

What are the stats of the players? Write them down.

_____
_____
_____
_____
_____
_____

What are your child's stats?

_____
_____
_____
_____

Would this be a good college to apply to based on your child's stats? Explain.

_____
_____
_____
_____
_____

Would this be a good college to apply based on your child's SAT/ACT scores and GPA? Explain. (Remember, student first, athlete second.)

_____
_____
_____
_____

What's the coach's name, email address and contact information?

_____

_____

_____

_____

Email the coach if you are interested and/or have your high school or organizational coach email them for you.

Have this information available before emailing them:

Your child's full name
Email address
Home Address
Telephone Number
NCAA # (if you have registered)
Know your stats!
An unedited video of your child playing in the game. (Do not pay expensive prices to have this done.)

_____

_____

_____

_____

If you are interested in the college, apply in your senior year. If you are accepted, send an email to the coach to let him/her know.

Scholarships may be available for Div. 1 and Div. 2 sports programs, but check with the college to make sure.

Scholarships may come in several ways. These scholarships must be renewed every year:

***Do not forget: You MUST complete the FAFSA form in order to receive NCAA scholarships & grants.** It's available Oct 1st of your child's senior year. **Check the FAFSA deadlines of all of your colleges to make sure you fill out the FAFSA form by that date.** It varies from college to college.*

Full Cost of Attendance (Tuition, Room & Board, Fees) may not include books.
How much is the Full Cost of Attendance for every college your child is thinking about?

_____

_____

_____

_____

_____

_____

_____

_____

_____

_____

Full or half of tuition (room and board, fees books are not included).

_____
_____
_____
_____
_____
_____

Some colleges may offer other combinations of funding, but may not be able to provide everything.

Make sure you know everything and read everything before you sign! Keep copies of everything for your records!

Write the names of the colleges that your child would like to apply to:

_____
_____
_____
_____
_____
_____
_____
_____
_____
_____
_____

What types of scholarships have been offered to my child? (Tuition, Room & Board, Fees, Other) and How much for each.

_____
_____
_____
_____
_____

What are names of the grants that have been offered to my child, if any?

_____
_____
_____
_____
_____

What are the names of the loans that have been offered to my child?

_____
_____
_____

How much will we/parents owe for the 1st year?

_____

_____

_____

_____

2nd year estimate?

_____

_____

_____

_____

3rd year estimate?

_____

_____

_____

_____

4th year estimate?

_____

_____

_____

_____

Have you completed the FAFSA form?

_____

_____

_____

What's your plan? What did you learn from this section?
Where, or with whom, do you need to talk to in this section? Explain and write your next steps.

_____

_____

_____

_____

_____

_____

_____

_____

_____

_____

_____

Additional Notes:

_____

_____

_____

_____

_____

_____

_____

_____

_____

_____

_____

_____

_____

_____

_____

_____

_____

_____

_____

_____

_____

Additional Notes:

Read Chapter 6

Finding The Right College

Here are websites that may help you plan for college:

Collegeboard.Com
Collegedata.Com
Collegeweeklive.Com

What type of college are you looking for?

_____
_____
_____
_____

What's your price range? Refer to this chapter if you are not sure.

_____
_____
_____
_____

In-State or Out of State Colleges?

_____
_____
_____
_____

Private or Public College?

_____
_____
_____
_____

Two-year or four-year College?

_____
_____
_____
_____

Now is the time for the Heart to Heart Conversation. Explain to your child how much you can afford to pay per year for college. Write it here!

_____

_____

_____

_____

Show your child the amount you can pay. Let your child know that anything above that amount will have to be awarded to them in the form of scholarships in order to attend that college.

For example: If the parent can pay $10,000 per year for college and the college costs $23,000, that means your child must bring in $13,000 per year in scholarships or grants and maybe a few thousand in loans in order to attend that college.

So here is Plan A, B, C & D:

Plan A *is that very expensive college that parents can't afford. Your child must receive a significant amount of scholarships that are* **renewable every year**. *You will pay the rest according to the amount you agreed to pay.*

Name the college(s) and the amount you can pay.

_____

_____

_____

_____

_____

_____

Plan B *is the less expensive four-year in-state or out-of-state college. The same agreement applies. Your child must receive a significant amount of scholarships that will be* **renewable every year**. *You will pay the rest according to the amount you agreed to pay.*

Name the college(s) and the amount you can pay.

_____

_____

_____

_____

_____

Plan C *is a two-year college in your area that is less expensive. Your child will transfer to the four-year college after completing two years at the community college. This also might be a four-year commuter college in your area that does not provide housing. The same agreement applies. Your child must still be expected to provide some type of scholarship or funding that will be* **renewable every year**. *You will pay the rest according to the amount you agreed to pay.*

Name the college(s) and the amount you can pay.

_____

_____

_____

_____

Plan D *- Student will work part time and go to college full time or vice versa. Name the college and the job that your child has or will have.*

_____
_____
_____
_____

How much as parent(s) can you afford to pay per year?

_____
_____
_____
_____

How much at an average will your child need in scholarships? (More detail will be provided in Chapter 8.)

_____
_____
_____
_____

What's Your Plan? What did you learn from this section?
Where or who do you need to follow up with in this section? Explain and write your next steps.

_____
_____
_____
_____
_____
_____
_____
_____
_____
_____
_____
_____
_____
_____
_____
_____
_____
_____
_____
_____

Parent <u>Only</u> Worksheet

Questions	Available options
Have you been on a <u>college tour</u> with your child?	☐ Yes ☐ No
Have you been to a <u>college fair</u> with your child?	☐ Yes ☐ No
Would you be willing to explore and attend college open houses around your city with your child?	☐ Yes ☐ No
Are you familiar with your child's current GPA?	☐ Yes ☐ No
Is your child involved in extra-curricular activities at school or in the community?	☐ Yes ☐ No
Given your budget, would you be able to afford private test prep sessions for your child?	☐ Yes ☐ No
Is your child eligible for a test fee waiver for the SAT and/or the ACT?	☐ Yes ☐ No
Would you prefer your child only considers SAT/ACT optional schools to reduce the cost of the prep?	☐ Yes ☐ No
If your child has taken a standardized test, did he or she earn college ready scores? Ask your child's counselor if you are unsure about this.	☐ Yes ☐ No
Would your child need to take the ESL Test for non-American English Speakers?	☐ Yes ☐ No
Would your child need to take the TOEFL should they go to a college or university?	☐ Yes ☐ No

This section has been provided courtesy of Dr. Stephanie Mbella, author of, "The Immigrant Guide to the American Educational System."

Provide your action plan below for any question answered "no" in the previous table.

_____

_____

_____

_____

_____

_____

_____

_____

_____

_____

_____

Key Points	Available Options		
Select all types of institutions you would like your child to attend.	□ In-state public school □ Out-of-state public school □ Out-of-state private school □ No preference	□ In-state private school □ Religious school □ Community College	
Do you have a specific college/university you would like your child to attend? Why or why not?	_____ _____ _____		
In the event your family cannot afford a four-year college tuition for your child, are you comfortable having the conversation about a community college as a viable option with them? Explain your answer.	_____ _____ _____ _____ _____		
Based on your family circumstances and your child's academic standing, select all types of aid he or she might be eligible for?	□ Need-based □ Athletics	□ Merit-based □ None	□ Work study □ I don't know
In the event your child cannot secure on campus housing, are you comfortable having them stay with roommates off-campus? Explain your answer.	_____ _____ _____ _____ _____		
Are there any special circumstances likely to affect your child's quality of life on campus? (Health, diet, and other important issues.)	_____ _____ _____ _____		
If you are a parent of an undocumented student, is the child aware of their legal status in the United States? If yes, list some of the schools to which he or she can apply. If no, how would you share this crucial piece of information with the child?	_____ _____ _____ _____ _____		
Please rate by order of importance to you the some of the college selection criteria	_____ Size _____ Alumni _____ Facilities _____ Location _____ Affiliation _____ Reputation _____ Student Life _____ Job Prospects _____ Tuition and Fees _____ Academic Support _____ Types of Enrollment _____ Available Financial Aid _____ Diversity of Student Body		

This section has been provided courtesy of Dr. Stephanie Mbella, author of, "The Immigrant Guide to the American Educational System."

Student Worksheet

Check all criteria you consider in your college selection process

Key Points	Available Options
Types of Colleges of Interest	☐ Public only ☐ Private only ☐ Both types ☐ I don't know
Institutions (Where do you want to attend college?)	☐ Two-year college (Community College or Junior College) ☐ Four-year college (University) ☐ Career school (Technical, Trade, Vocational) _____ *Specify*
Location	☐ In-state only ☐ Out- of- state only ☐ Both ☐ Metropolitan area ☐ Urban area ☐ Rural area
Academics	☐ Reputation of the school ☐ Number of majors of study ☐ Faculty-student ratio ☐ Library size ☐ Laboratory and equipment ☐ Tutoring centers ☐ Math help centers ☐ Writing center ☐ Lab assistance ☐ Special accommodations
Size and enrollment	☐ Large size campus ☐ Medium size campus ☐ Small size campus ☐ All female campus ☐ All male campus ☐ Co-educational campus
Financial cost	☐ Tuition and fees ☐ Room and board ☐ Books and supplies
Available aid	☐ Need-based aid ☐ Merit-based aid ☐ Work stud ☐ Specialized scholarships: _____ ☐ R.O.T.C *Specify major*
Other considerations	☐ Athletic activities ☐ Career Center ☐ Diversity of the student body (Ethnic minorities: HBCU / HACU) ☐ Family and friends ☐ Internship opportunities ☐ Religion ☐ Study abroad programs

This section has been provided courtesy of Dr. Stephanie Mbella, author of, "The Immigrant Guide to the American Educational System."

College Application Process

Parent and Student Worksheet
Please complete together.

Key Points	Available Options
What college admission type (s) is your child considering?	□ Early Decision □ Early Action □ Restricted Early Action □ Regular Admission □ Rolling Admission
Select all information accessible to your child for the college application process	□ Child social security number □ Child immigration status □ Parent date of birth □ Parent (s) educational level □ Parent divorce/separation date □ Parent's occupation □ Parent's employer □ Siblings dates of birth □ Siblings ages □ Siblings educational levels
Is your child eligible for a fee waiver?	□ Yes □ No □ I don't know
If yes, what organization provided the college application fee waivers?	
How many college fee waivers is your child eligible for?	
Is your child enrolled in a college readiness program? Ask your child's counselor.	□ Yes □ No □ I don't know
If yes, when was the last time you met as a team?	
When was the last time you had a college planning meeting your child's counselor?	
Does the school provide help to students in paying for AP Exams in May?	□ Yes □ No □ I don't know

This section has been provided courtesy of Dr. Stephanie Mbella, author of, "The Immigrant Guide to the American Educational System."

Student Worksheet

Complete the following table to estimate the cost of your college applications.

#	College	State	College Categories (R, T, S)	Application Types (SA, CA, CAAS)	Admission Types (ED, EA, ERA, RED, ROA)	Application Deadline	Fee
1							
2							
3							
4							
5							
6							
7							
8							
9							
10							
11							
12							
13							
14							
15						Total Cost:	

C Categories:

R= Reach School   T= Target School   S= Safety

Application Types:

SA= School App   CA= Common App   CAAS= Coalition App

Admission Types:

ED= Early Decision   EA = Early Action   ERA= Early Restricted Action
RED= Regular Decision   ROA= Rolling Admission

This section has been provided courtesy of Dr. Stephanie Mbella, author of, "The Immigrant Guide to the American Educational System."

Parent and Student Worksheet

Complete the following table to estimate your college application budget.

Items	Fee per Unit	Number of Units	Total Cost
SAT Test (s) with writing			
ACT Test (s) with writing			
AP Test (s)			
College 1 - Application fee			
College 2 - Application fee			
College 3 - Application fee			
College 4 - Application fee			
College 5 - Application fee			
College 6 - Application fee			
College 7 - Application fee			
College 8 - Application fee			
College 9 - Application fee			
College 10 - Application fee			
Submission of SAT Scores to College (s)			
Submission of ACT Scores to College (s)			
Submission of Transcripts to College (s)			
Enrollment Security Deposit			
Housing Security Deposit			
		Estimated Budget:	

This section has been provided courtesy of Dr. Stephanie Mbella, author of, "The Immigrant Guide to the American Educational System."

Additional Notes:

_____

_____

_____

_____

_____

_____

_____

_____

_____

_____

_____

_____

_____

_____

_____

_____

_____

_____

_____

_____

_____

_____

_____

Additional Notes:

Read Chapter 7

Get To Know Your Child's Counselor!

It's important to meet with your child's counselor once or twice a year unless more meetings are required due to IEPs (Individualized Educational Program) or 504 plans. Teachers can be invited to the meeting at your request.

What's the name of your child's counselor?

_____

_____

_____

What's the date and time of your appointment?

_____

_____

_____

_____

Questions you may want to ask:

If your child has an IEP or 504, is it up to date?

_____

_____

_____

_____

If your child has an IEP or 504, ask your counselor if your child can receive accommodations (that could mean extra time or other modifications) on SAT/ACT tests.

If the answer is Yes, what needs to be done by your counselor and how will you be notified when it has been completed? Write that information here!

_____

_____

_____

_____

_____

_____

_____

_____

_____

College Planning with your Counselor and/or College Counselor (High school students 9th -12th grade)

Is there a list of colleges that are sending representatives to my child's school during the day? Write down the names of colleges that your child may be interested in.

_____
_____
_____
_____
_____

What college fairs are coming to the area? Does the school provide transportation to any college fairs?

_____
_____
_____
_____
_____
_____
_____

What colleges would you recommend for my child based on his/her interests and academic profile?

_____
_____
_____
_____
_____
_____
_____
_____

Do you know of any scholarships or scholarship websites we can search? Have any scholarships come into your office that my child may apply?

_____
_____
_____
_____
_____
_____

Do you know of any special scholarships that colleges are offering that meet my child's academic profile and interests? (It's always good to know this even if your child is not a senior yet.)

_____
_____
_____
_____
_____
_____

Looking at my child's courses, would you suggest making changes to their schedule to be more competitive to colleges? Write this down!

_____
_____
_____
_____
_____
_____
_____

How many credits will my child have when/she graduates? How many do they have now, and are they on target for graduation?

_____
_____
_____
_____
_____
_____

Based on my child's academic strengths, would you suggest Honors or AP classes?

_____
_____
_____
_____
_____

Is my child ready for Honors AP or IB courses (Advanced Placement/College Level, International Baccalaureate)?

If so, are there additional tutoring programs or other support for students who take these classes? Write this down specifically, or have the counselor/teacher email you so that you have it in writing.

_____
_____
_____
_____
_____
_____
_____

When it comes to AP exams, should my child take them? What's the benefit of taking an AP exam?

_____
_____
_____
_____
_____

Should my child take the AP exam right after completing the course while it's still fresh in their mind?

_____

_____

_____

_____

_____

Should my child consider dual enrollment classes in his/her senior year of school at a college that has partnered with our school, if this is available?

_____

_____

_____

_____

_____

_____

_____

Do you know of any internships or summer programs that may be available for my child?

_____

_____

_____

_____

_____

_____

_____

Do you have a list of organizations that provide community service hours for students?

_____

_____

_____

_____

_____

_____

_____

What's your plan? What did you learn from this section?
Where, or with whom, do you need to talk to in this section? Explain and write your next steps.

_____

_____

_____

_____

_____

_____

Additional Notes:

_____

_____

_____

_____

_____

_____

_____

_____

_____

_____

_____

_____

_____

_____

_____

_____

_____

_____

Additional Notes:

_____

_____

_____

_____

_____

_____

_____

_____

_____

_____

_____

_____

_____

_____

_____

_____

_____

_____

_____

_____

Read Chapter 8

Scholarships

Yes, there are a lot of scholarships available! You need a plan of action to obtain them. Parents, you **MUST** *be involved or find someone who can assist your child! Scholarships may be available for all grade levels, especially high school. Don't wait until your child's senior year to start researching!*

Follow the suggestions in this chapter!

Register free of charge to fastweb.com, scholarships.org, finaid.com or other scholarship websites. You should not have to pay to register, so beware!

Write down your username and password in a safe place.

Have an email address for you and your child that YOU will have access to. You will need to check this periodically if your child doesn't.

What are the requirements of the scholarship?

_____
_____
_____
_____
_____

Does your child meet the requirements of the scholarship?

_____
_____
_____
_____

What's the deadline date to apply for the scholarship?

_____
_____
_____
_____

Is an essay required? What's the topic of the essay?

_____
_____
_____

Who will assist your child with the essay?

_____
_____
_____
_____

Recommendation letters:

Ask teachers and counselors at least two-three weeks BEFORE the scholarship deadline so that they have time to write it. You may have to provide teachers/counselors with additional information about your child before a recommendation letter can be requested.

If your child needs a recommendation letter, when will you request it?

_____
_____

Write down the date your child requested the recommendation letter.

_____
_____
_____
_____

Does your child need to provide additional information to the teacher? If so, what?

_____
_____
_____
_____
_____
_____

If your child needs a Counselor recommendation letter, when will you request it?

_____
_____
_____

Write down the date you requested the counselor recommendation letter.

_____
_____
_____

Does your child need to provide additional information to the teacher? If so, what?

_____
_____
_____
_____
_____

Mailing the scholarship application:

Do you have all of the documents ready to mail?

Completed Application? _____

Essay? _____

Recommendation Letters? _____

*Official Transcript? (ask counselor or registrar at least 1 week prior)*_____

Other documents requested? _____

Is the scholarship being mailed at the post office? _____

If so, who will take it to the post office? _____

Do you have 9x12 large envelopes to put all of the documents in?

_____

Have you addressed the envelope correctly? _____

Have you added your return address? _____

Do you have postage stamps? If so, how many? _____

If applying online, everything may have to be uploaded at the same time (note: teachers may not give the student their recommendation letters or transcript to mail). Ask how these items will be sent. Most schools will send them directly to the scholarship organization or company.

Do not wait until the deadline date to mail your application! Remember, the old saying, "the early bird gets the worm!"

_____
_____
_____
_____
_____
_____
_____

What's your plan? What did you learn from this section?
Where, or with whom, do you need to talk to in this section? Explain and write your next steps.

_____
_____
_____
_____
_____

Additional Notes:

Additional Notes:

_____

_____

_____

_____

_____

_____

_____

_____

_____

_____

_____

_____

_____

_____

_____

_____

_____

_____

_____

_____

Read Chapter 9

FAFSA – Free Application for Federal Student Aid

Most of this section is for parents of High School Seniors, however, parents who have middle or high school students, please go to this website to see an estimate of what you may have to pay for college per year. You will need a copy of your most recent taxes to complete it. https://bigfuture.collegeboard.org/pay-for-college/paying-your-share/ expected-family-contribution-calculator

The FAFSA form can only be filled out by high school seniors and one parent. You can start filling out the form on Oct 1st of your child's senior year of high school. Getting assistance with this form is strongly suggested. Check with your counseling department for more information about organizations or individuals who will be able to assist you with this form.

If you are a U.S. citizen or permanent resident, you should fill out this form regardless of how much you make. Fill it out! This form will be required every year your child is in college. There may be other financial aid forms to complete as well.

Who will assist you with filling out this form?

_____
_____
_____
_____
_____
_____

What's the financial aid deadline date for all the colleges your child is applying?

_____
_____
_____
_____
_____
_____
_____
_____
_____
_____
_____
_____
_____
_____

Do you have all of the required documents to fill out the form?

Previous year's tax forms _____

Social Security Numbers of Parents _____

Social Security Number of Student _____

Bank Statements may be needed _____
Other Assets _____

When you are ready to fill out the form, go to the fafsa.gov or fafsa.ed.gov website. (These are the ONLY websites. It's free! If you are on a website that's charging you a fee, get off the website!

You and your child will need a Federal Student Aid (FSA ID Number).

Keep all of this information in a safe place. You will need it every year!

FSA ID Student Username/Email: _____
FSA ID Parent Username/Email: _____

Student Password: _____

Parent Password: _____

Student's Answers to FSA ID Questions:

_____
_____
_____
_____
_____

Parent's Answers to FSA ID Questions:

_____
_____
_____
_____
_____

What's your plan? What did you learn from this section?
Where or who do you need to follow up with in this section? Explain and write your next steps.

_____
_____
_____
_____
_____

Additional Information:

_____

_____

_____

_____

_____

_____

_____

_____

_____

_____

_____

_____

_____

_____

_____

_____

_____

_____

_____

_____

Additional Notes:

_____

_____

_____

_____

_____

_____

_____

_____

_____

_____

_____

_____

_____

_____

_____

_____

_____

_____

_____

_____

_____

Paying for College Parent and Student Worksheet

Complete together to create a timeline to complete your financial aid forms.

	School	State	FAFSA Priority Deadline	CSS Priority Deadline (if applicable)	State Aid Priority Deadline
1					
2					
3					
4					
5					
6					
7					
8					
9					
10					
11					
12					

This section has been provided courtesy of Dr. Stephanie Mbella, author of, "The Immigrant Guide to the American Educational System."

Parent and Student Worksheet Elements of a Financial Aid Package

Using the financial aid estimator of all colleges you are considering, complete the following table as much as you can. Bear in mind that not all information will be immediately available to you.

College	COA (Cost of Attendance)	EFC (Expected Family Contribution)	Financial Aid Package					Total Awards	Gap between COA and EFC = Parents Contribution
			Pell Grant	Subsidized Loan	Unsubsidized Loan	Scholarships	Work Study		

This section has been provided courtesy of Dr. Stephanie Mbella, author of, "The Immigrant Guide to the American Educational System."

Parent and Student Worksheet

Compare College Costs to determine your best financially fit school.

Name of College	College 1	College 2	College 3	College 4	College 5
Tuition					
Fees					
Room (Dorm)					
Board (Meal Plan)					
Books & Supplies					
Health Insurance					
Appliances					
Cellphone Service					
Computer/Laptop					
Bedding					
Clothing					
Groceries					
Transportation					
Personal expenses					
Entertainment					
Total Annual Cost of Attendance					

Rate your 3 best financially fit schools

1_____ 2_____ 3_____

This section has been provided courtesy of Dr. Stephanie Mbella, author of, "The Immigrant Guide to the American Educational System."

Sample College Applications Tracker

School & State	Admission Types	Categories	Application Types	Date Transcript Requests Submitted	Date Recommendation Letters Submitted	Date ACT Scores sent to Colleges	Date SAT Scores sent to Colleges	Date Application submitted to College	Date Application Fee Waiver or Payment sent to Colleges

Admission Types:

ED = Early Decision   EA = Earlier Action   ERA = Early Restricted Action   RD = Regular Decision   ROA = Rolling Admission

School Categories: R = Reach School   T = Target School   S = Safety School

Application Types: SA = School Application   CA = Common Application   CAAS = Coalition Application

Optional requirements:

-    Date Mid-Year Report sent to Colleges: _____

-    Date TOEFL Scores sent to Colleges: _____

This section has been provided courtesy of Dr. Stephanie Mbella, author of, "The Immigrant Guide to the American Educational System."

Sample Financial Aid Application Tracker

Date CSS Profile Submitted at Schools (if applicable)	FAFSA Submission Date	SAR (Student Aid Report) Reception Date	Date IRS Data Retrieval Tool Completed (if applicable)	Date State Grant Application Submitted (if applicable)	Date Senators Scholarship Applications Submitted (if applicable)	Date Delegates Scholarship Applications Submitted (if applicable)

73

This section has been provided courtesy of Dr. Stephanie Mbella, author of, "The Immigrant Guide to the American Educational System."

Sample Scholarship Applications Tracker

Name of Scholarship	Types Merit-based Need-based Athletic-based Community Service Other	Organization/ Sponsor/ Administrator	Contacts for questions	Award Amount	Submission Deadline	Date Application Submitted

This section has been provided courtesy of Dr. Stephanie Mbella, author of, "The Immigrant Guide to the American Educational System."

Read Chapter 10

How to Find the Best Colleges for Your Buck

If you live in a state that is part of the Academic Common Market, read this chapter and following the instructions in the book or go to SREB.ORG for more information.

If you do not live in any of the states of the Academic Common Market, you may live in The Western Interstate Commission area. Check out wiche.edu.

If you are in any of these states, list the colleges in other states that provide a discount for your child. If you are unsure, check with your child's counseling department.

List the colleges in other states that provide discount tuition for students in your state. How much will you save?

_____
_____
_____
_____
_____
_____
_____
_____
_____
_____
_____
_____
_____
_____
_____
_____
_____
_____
_____
_____
_____
_____
_____
_____
_____
_____

What's your plan? What did you learn from this section?
Where, or with whom, do you need to talk to in this section? Explain and write your next steps.

_____
_____
_____
_____
_____
_____
_____
_____
_____
_____
_____
_____
_____
_____
_____
_____
_____
_____
_____
_____
_____
_____
_____
_____
_____
_____
_____
_____

Additional Information:

_____

_____

_____

_____

_____

_____

_____

_____

_____

_____

_____

_____

_____

_____

_____

_____

_____

_____

_____

_____

Additional Information:

_____

_____

_____

_____

_____

_____

_____

_____

_____

_____

_____

_____

_____

_____

_____

_____

_____

_____

_____

Read Chapter 11

Counting up the Cost!

This is so important. Using the examples in this chapter, write down how much you spend, daily, weekly and yearly and times that number by 18 years to see how much you may be able to save for college! This is just an estimate, of course, but may provide you with an idea of how much you can save for college:

How much do you spend weekly on snacks, fast food, coffee, etc. What about cell phone costs?

Add it up!

_____
_____
_____
_____
_____
_____
_____
_____
_____
_____
_____

Following the example in Chapter 11, If you saved $5- $25 per week how much could you save in 18 years, or the years left, before your child graduates from high school?

Add it up!

_____
_____
_____
_____
_____
_____
_____
_____
_____
_____
_____

What's your plan? What did you learn from this section?
Where, or with whom, do you need to talk to in this section? Explain and write your next steps.

_____
_____
_____
_____
_____
_____
_____
_____
_____
_____
_____
_____
_____
_____
_____
_____
_____
_____
_____
_____
_____
_____
_____
_____
_____
_____
_____
_____
_____
_____
_____
_____
_____

Additional Notes:

_____

_____

_____

_____

_____

_____

_____

_____

_____

_____

_____

_____

_____

_____

_____

_____

_____

_____

_____

Additional Notes:

Read Chapter 12

Professional Judgment and Appeal Letters

After reading this chapter, if you feel that you have a professional judgment or would like to write an appeal letter to your child's college, write it out here, first. Not all colleges will provide more scholarship money, but it's worth asking.

Here are a few things that may be a good reason to write an appeal letter so that colleges can make a professional judgment:

- *Loss of job*
- *High medical bills*
- *Taking care of older parents*
- *High cost of private school tuition*
- *High cost of living in a "good school district"*
- *Recent death of a spouse*
- *Decrease in income*
- *Large increase in income*

These are just a few. There could be more reasons why your income has changed drastically.

Make sure you have documentation in case you are asked to provide proof.

What's your plan? What did you learn from this section?
Where or who do you need to follow up with in this section? Explain and write your next steps.

_____

_____

_____

_____

_____

_____

_____

_____

_____

_____

_____

_____

_____

_____

_____

_____

_____

_____

Additional Notes:

Additional Notes:

_____

_____

_____

_____

_____

_____

_____

_____

_____

_____

_____

_____

_____

_____

_____

_____

_____

_____

_____

_____

_____

_____

Read Chapter 13

Moms and Dads: Always Keep a Tissue Handy!

I remember this like it was yesterday. I cried for nearly an hour! I had no idea what I would do without my children. It was hard at first, but we got over it!

Think about what you will do when you and your spouse have an "empty nest," no children at home for a while!

What will you do with your time? Travel? Go back to School? Start or continuing working on a hobby? Get involved in your community and/or place of worship? Find your passion and work it!

What's your plan? What did you learn from this section?
Where or who do you need to follow up with in this section? Explain and write your next steps.

_____
_____
_____
_____
_____
_____
_____
_____
_____
_____
_____
_____
_____
_____
_____
_____
_____
_____
_____
_____
_____
_____

Additional Notes:

_____

_____

_____

_____

_____

_____

_____

_____

_____

_____

_____

_____

_____

_____

_____

_____

_____

_____

_____

_____

Additional Notes:

Additional Notes:

_____

_____

_____

_____

_____

_____

_____

_____

_____

_____

_____

_____

_____

_____

_____

_____

_____

_____

_____

_____

_____

Additional Notes:

_____

_____

_____

_____

_____

_____

_____

_____

_____

_____

_____

_____

_____

_____

_____

_____

_____

_____

_____

_____

_____

Additional Notes:

_____

_____

_____

_____

_____

_____

_____

_____

_____

_____

_____

_____

_____

_____

_____

_____

_____

_____

_____

Additional Notes:

_____

_____

_____

_____

_____

_____

_____

_____

_____

_____

_____

_____

_____

_____

_____

_____

_____

_____

_____